Preface

I am not a medical doctor. maker and formulator of natural products for people with sensitive skin. This is the story of what I've learned over the past twenty years as I attempted to live, cope and thrive with MY Reactive Body. It contains real advice to help YOU to thrive in YOUR Reactive Body too – each day, every day, the rest of your hopefully long and happy time here.

I believe that the Reactive Body mechanism is a natural phenomenon and that it would not exist of it was not supposed to be here in the first place. A Reactive Body delivers the messages we were not listening to first ten times before. It can save us from exposure to tumor enhancing substances and to asthma triggers that we probably do not want to be exposed to anyway. A Reactive Body mechanism can save your life, but living with a Reactive Body turned on "high" all the time can destroy it. That is why it is so important to take a multi-faceted approach to the treatment of this poorly understood disease.

Think of it as being in training. You are in training to resist Reactive Body flare-ups. You do this by taking and rotating your tonics; getting lots of fresh air, clean water and moderate sunlight; eating fresh, colorful food grown in rich, organic soil so it is full of nutrition; and controlling and systematically reducing stress and the cascade of stress hormones that attack your body. You must do the work consciously every day as you exercise your body, control and focus your mind, and optimize your nutrition. You must continuously work at eliminating non-nutritious, empty calories and artificial chemical food additives from your dietary intake while reducing exposure to trigger molecules.

There are some great coping strategies in this book that will help you to reduce and shorten flare-up reactions so you can get on with your day more or less in peace. These Reactive Body coping strategies include mental and emotional centering tools for your reactive mind, and physical and molecular tools for your reactive body. The beauty of these coping strategies is that they just take a minute to do, they use what is around you, and they cost basically nothing but your time and awareness.

This book was written for you, the person with a Reactive Body. But, it was also written for all the people who love you and struggle to live with your molecular sensitivities so they can better understand their effect on your overall health and emotional stability. You do not have to destroy your life and the things you work so hard for to learn Life's Lessons. You just have to learn to listen.

Chapter 1

My Reactive Body

Hello. My name is Larry and I have a Reactive Body.

In 1991 my body went through a breakdown of sorts. In a short period of time I became highly sensitized or intolerant to most artificial scents, many artificial colors, propylene glycol, and many aromatic and petrochemical products, including most plastics. I went to a specialist complaining about these newfound chemical "allergies". The doctor bristled at my ignorance.

"An allergy," he explained, "is a protein antibody created in reaction to a protein invader inside your body." None of the chemicals on my list contained proteins.

The specialist recommended a scratch test. A nurse made a hundred or more fine scratches on my back and placed a drop of a contaminant onto each scratch. If there was a visible reaction to one of the contaminants in the scratch test, one could be pretty sure a protein antibody was present. This was a useful – if uncomfortable – exercise. At the end of the ordeal, I found out that I was highly allergic to dust and dust mites. This was good information, but the allergists couldn't help me with the chemical sensitivity issues at all.

The doctors were perfectly happy prescribing inhalers and antihistamine pills and steroids to help control my dust mite allergy. A friend of mine thought better of it and cautioned: "You can always go back to the doctors; they'll be happy to take your money. And besides, something like 40% of us are allergic to dust mites. Somehow we all survive."

On his advice I bought a box of high quality dust masks and upgraded my vacuum cleaner. I began to avoid dusty jobs and dusty areas. These changes helped the dust issues immensely but did nothing to help with the chemical intolerances I was experiencing. I did notice that when I was "dusted", or over-exposed to dust, I was also more sensitive to fragrances and skin irritants. This actually made sense. Dust mites secrete poisons that make our bodies more reactive than they would normally be. After "being dusted" it seemed as if my overall natural resistance was sapped and I felt drained. This run-down state left me more reactive to things I could normally shrug off, like petrochemical based odors.

It dawned on me that there is actually little understanding or even research about the causes, mechanisms and treatment of Reactive Bodies. Nor should I expect any major breakthroughs anytime soon.

I felt very alone inside my Reactive Body.

Tired of feeling depressed and broken, I decided to become my own molecular detective – an amateur Sherlock Holmes uncovering my true **chemical triggers**, as well as the **tonics** and **antidotes** for my Reactive Body symptoms. I needed to learn what molecules increased or decreased my **immune system buffer**.

And this is exactly what YOU have to do.

YOU have to put on your Sherlock Holmes hat and become a molecular detective. YOU have to figure out what YOUR triggers are; what sets you off into a tailspin. I recommend reading this book and then finding a very good Naturopathic Physician that specializes in this type of work. Don't expect miracles. Just listen to what they say and, if it doesn't involve using a lot of drugs, give their advice some weight.

Whatever path you take **do not expect anyone but you** to be able to do the daily work of peeling back the layers of your environmental sensitivities and reactions. You have to discover how you manifest YOUR symptoms, and what the best tonics and antidotes are to build up your body and keep it strong.

How to do your own Patch Test

Did you know that the most sensitive skin on the human body is located on the inner elbow?

On one elbow (leave the other for comparison) gently and briefly rub the product you want to test onto your skin. If it is a lotion or cosmetic this is easy. If it is a bar soap or something dry, wet the substance first.

A strong reaction occurs almost instantly, usually in the form of a raised welt. Mild reactions can take up to 2 hours to occur and might manifest as white or red bumps, mildly rash-y, flushing in the area with itchy skin.

If you have a very mild reaction repeat the experiment several times on different days when you are feeling strong and when you are feeling weak. This will give you a good idea how to relate to that particular substance.

If you have a strong immediate reaction note all the ingredients in the product and attempt to Sherlock Holmes which molecules are triggers for you.

Chapter 2

What is a Reactive Body?

You know the old practice of bringing canaries down into coal mines? Mining (coal mining especially) can release large amounts of the natural gas methane. Methane displaces the air we breathe. Without necessary amounts of oxygen from that air, humans are toast in a matter of minutes. The canaries, brought down to sing as the miners worked, are more sensitive to the drop in oxygen level than humans. They would be the first to suffer from the lack of oxygen, and stop singing. This gave the miners a couple of minutes notice to get the heck out of Dodge and possibly save their coal mining lives. Reactive Body people are like those sleeping canaries. We notice molecules before other people do.

Reactive Bodies feel and perceive the world more intensely than most. This hyped up sensitivity increases the risk of becoming over stimulated and exhausted; and thus short-tempered with those we love. You hear that? *Reactive Bodies are easily over stimulated because they feel the world more intensely.* A Reactive Body is not a psychosomatic illness as some people, and even many professionals, believe. If they had a Reactive Body, they would not talk so foolishly!

Having a Reactive Body is kind of like having Body Asthma. Asthma is by definition a pulmonary condition characterized by inflammation of the bronchial lining, but a Reactive Body is essentially a body in which every part and system has the potential for inflammation and hypersensitivity. When something molecular triggers you, you may experience a **flare-up**, which may or may not include: histamine-based reactions; hypersensitivity to aromas; mood swings, including bipolar behaviors; anxiety or panic; and general hypersensitivity to anything that might pose a threat to your metabolic wellbeing and balance. The flare-up eventually subsides, but the hypersensitivity may linger for days. After a flare-up you are left feeling spent and emotionally rung out.

I believe that Reactive Bodies are following a normal human mechanism. For example, you know when someone has overindulged in an alcohol product and they can no longer stand to drink or even smell that type of liquor any more?

"No (tequila, rum, whiskey, etc.) for me ever!"

They had a big night on it once and got very sick. Now their body cannot even stand the smell of it. I have known people to get nauseous just from talking about it. This is the same principal as a Reactive Body response. It is a body's way of saying, "I told you when I made you sneeze; I told you when I made you cough; I told you when I gave you a headache. I told you over and over, but now I am telling you **under no uncertain terms to listen up and stop exposing yourself to this particular molecular trigger!**"

How the heck did I end up with this Reactive Body?

That's a great question, but there are a million ways to answer it. You may have a Reactive Body that is the result of, or worsened by, a food allergy. Your Reactive Body may be a result of Lyme disease, or some other disease or parasite that chronically weakens your body. It may be tied to long-term exposure to mold, or to metals, or workplace solvent exposure, or to too much chalkboard eraser dust in the first grade. Some studies suggest that childhood exposure to cigarette smoke and to organophosphate pesticides is linked to becoming a Reactive Body later in life. You may even have been born Reactive as a result of shared exposure

Coping Strategy

It's not that I am broken; this stuff really IS bad for me!

Repeat this to yourself – it will help you to feel better:

It's not that I am broken; this stuff really IS bad for me!

You might as well say it twice - louder!

It's not that I am broken; this stuff really IS bad for me!

Then run for fresh air if you need to.

9

(including legal pharmaceuticals) with your mother.

There are people who swear that their personal trauma is what caused them to now have Reactive Bodies. I believe them. Few people take the car out every day and never get a scratch or a dent or a quirk in the works. And precious few of us make it to adulthood without facing outrageous insult and scarring.

Let's flow chart out one possible scenario:

- Egregious Insult >>

- Cascade of Corticoids (stress hormones) >>

- Changes the way NMDA cells process glutamates* >>

- Raises the voltage of electricity running through your body >>

- Body becomes prone to episodic hyper-sensitization (flare-ups) >>

- Recurrent PTSD flashes re-trigger the endocrine system stress cascade>>

- Starting the process over again.

  * (to be discussed in Chapter 3)

Now, an egregious insult by itself is not enough to create a Reactive Body. Other environmental factors must also be present, like organophosphate pesticide exposure, or metal poisoning, or ongoing exposure to petrochemical solvents coupled with a candida yeast infection, or two out of the three.

Along with a host of other potential contaminates, these exposures USE UP our immune system buffer (liver health and overall élan), which leaves us vulnerable and open to hypersensitivity flare-ups.

Recipe for Disaster

Start with one compromised immune system that has experienced pesticide exposure in childhood. Combine with ongoing corticoid over-exposure (extreme stress). Place in a pressure cooker i.e. life and wait a few years. Voila!

Now, I am not saying that this combination will produce a Reactive Body every time, but what I am saying is that if you want to create a Reactive Body, this is a really good way to go about it.

It's not too good for your arteries either.

I became chemical sensitive after seven years of exposure to common cleaning chemicals when I worked as a commercial high rise window cleaner twenty plus years ago. During this time I knew that I was an "adrenaline junkie". My professional job was to jump off buildings. I had no idea what I was doing to my arteries, or what the cleaning chemicals were doing to my liver. There I was, being inundated with synthetic cleaning chemicals while my body was hyped up on its own adrenaline and stress

The Candida Connection

Candida Albicans is kind of like bread mold that can run amok in your belly. It lives on the surface of fruits and berries and we all have it in us.

This is not normally an issue in a healthy belly. However, antibiotics are broad spectrum, killing the good help-you-to-digest-your-food bacteria along with the bad ones trying to so hard to kill you. The hypothesis is that candida will set out runners, like bread mold does, and that these runners can work their way into your villi, eventually perforating the intestine and

hormones while fighting off a long running *candida* yeast infection. Certainly there is multiple causality present in my case. But does this hypothesis hold up over a large and diverse range of test subjects?

Time will tell.

However you got here, the road ahead will become clearer as you work through the layers of your symptoms and reactions to the environmental (molecular) roots of your issues.

Being Scentsitive

Wouldn't it be nice to have a magic machine that could sense all the bad, airborne molecule triggers that make you flare-up? Maybe something small and portable you could carry around with you everywhere, without attracting attention? Well guess what – you already have one! **Your nose is a powerful chemical sensor** and it's very happy to smell out toxic molecules for you. A little work on aromatic database building and before you know it you will have permanent access to a molecular motion detector that no machine yet devised can come close to matching!

As I was learning what my fragrance triggers were, I told people I was "sensitive" to smells. This just got me a lot of dirty looks. Sometimes people moved away from me, which was actually better because I didn't have to smell their cheap toiletries anymore. Believe me, telling people you are sensitive to something just confuses them.

Now, when I found out I have asthma everything changed. Tell the hostess in a restaurant that you have asthma and they will move tables around to put you by a window. The last thing they need is to have to call 911 in the middle of their lunch rush. Tell them you are sensitive and they will recommend

allowing food molecules to break the blood barrier. This of course could trigger an allergic response and a resulting food allergy for life.

Candida will also pump out toxic substances that can depress your immune system and your energy level. Candida over running your belly may possibly be a factor in the creation of Reactive Bodies. It will certainly be working against you as you work to keep yourself healthy and trying to avoid flare ups.

the artistic place up the road (which might not be such a bad idea anyway).

Since so many people have asthma and the majority of the population understands it, it's easy to casually explain your symptoms this way instead of trying to explain your Reactive Body condition. Imagine you're in the midst of a flare-up, and your friends and family are telling someone, "Sorry, she has asthma. Fake scents drive her crazy." It's not, "Oh that's just my mom. She's decided she's allergic to her shampoo today."

It is very easy to be dismissed as a kook if you are not careful. Telling someone you are chemically sensitive does not tell him or her the breadth and depth of your condition. You do not want to be the "Oh, she's just crazy" person when you are in the middle of a reactive flare-up.

If you ARE "scentsitive" you probably are at least mildly asthmatic. Feel comfortable excusing yourself when you cannot tolerate someone's fragrance preferences. Survival is Job #1. Let people know that you are asthmatic and that you are sometimes triggered by scents. Tell them your inhaler is in the car and leave quickly and politely before you can't take any more.

Teenagers are the hardest people of all to deal with. They may not voluntarily change their behavior until they see you having a near-death experience and have to personally peel you off the floor; but it can be done. Stinky teen cologne that masks any natural human aroma is popular at a certain age. Ban these from the house. The sooner you start, the safer your home will become, but be sure of your olfactory triggers before you speak.

Do nearly ALL artificial scents bother you? You may well have a toluene trigger. Start introducing unscented products into your home. Unscented mass-market products are a step in the right direction, but natural and organic ones are truly your best and safest bet.

It is very hard to quickly identify every chemical trigger in crappy quality (sorry – mass-market quality) products. You are much better off buying the highest quality natural and organic products you can find. Look for the ones with the fewest ingredients and make sure that you can pronounce them all.

Unfortunately even then there is a chance you are being tricked with "greenwashing' marketing words! A high price tag is not always a guarantee of naturalness. Learn to be a label reader – to understand what the molecules in the formula do to the product and what they could do to you!

Chapter 3
Science and the Reactive Body

You need to become comfortable looking at the world as a place built from little bricks called molecules. Humans are made up of an eternal and ever changing molecular soup. When we die, the molecular portion of our being will return to the soup from which it came, only to resurface as building blocks in other life forms. Nothing is wasted; nothing is lost. Pretty cool huh? We don't always stop and realize that our bodies are part and parcel of the carbon molecular soup that came before, and will come again and again and again.

Keeps you humble.

Our bodies can process, break down and rearrange tens of thousands of molecules and molecular combinations. Fortunately, most of this occurs automatically, freeing our minds for much more important work like art, philosophy and soap making.

But human minds are restless minds. Not content with a formulation kit consisting of the tens of thousands of molecules and molecular combinations found in nature, modern chemists began creating and working with new and novel chemicals that never or rarely appear naturally on the face of the earth. Within a hundred years the proliferation of these new and novel petroleum-, uranium-, and metal-based molecules have spread across the entire planet at a pace that can only be described as staggering. Each day millions of tons of novel and exotic molecules are poured into the air we breathe, the water we drink, the food we eat, the medicines we use. We rub them into our hair and skin. Remember that scratch test I talked about earlier? Rubbing fragrance, cleaning and preservative molecules into your skin is like doing a giant scratch test on yourself. No wonder so many people have skin issues!

Science has no clear idea what the long-term consequences of this molecular assault will be on ourselves, our planet, or the ecosystems that sustain us. We, the consumers of the world, are (mostly without our consent) part of a suicidal, multi-generational, planetary experiment; an experiment that probably will not stop until there is a 100% chance that every citizen will break out with cancer in their lifetime. Since the current rate is about 65% right now, we do not have that far to go.

I mention cancer because it is directly related to Reactive Bodies. Many (but certainly not all) of the chemical triggers that effect chemically sensitized people are known or suspected to be linked to increased risk of cancerous tumors in mammals. The majority of these chemicals and chemical combinations did not exist even one hundred years ago!

Ostensibly, the greater the amount of cancer trigger molecules you are exposed to, the greater the risk of your body coming out with cancer. You come **down** with a cold. But you come **out** with cancer. There is a subtle difference. Cancer is an environmental disease and, unfortunately, some genes (but only in 6% of cases) seem to make one more susceptible to it. Makes plain sense that your body wants to tell you to stay away from them!

The Science Behind a Reactive Body

Reactive Body people are sometimes described as "lit up", "intense" and "110% all the time". I would put forth that they often are exactly that.

Spread throughout your nervous system are nerve-regulating cells called NMDA or N-methyl-D-aspartate receptor cells. These cells are like a dimmer switch on a lamp that brightens or darkens with a turn of a knob. NMDA cells can potentially increase or decrease the amount of electricity traveling through your nerves by up to 50%!

NMDA cells are covered with glutamate receptors and calcium receptors that tell the cell to open or close the valve. Flood the cells with glutamates – monosodium glutamate (MSG) for example – and those NMDA cells can turn the valve wide open. This pours more electricity in your system, which means more… everything! It's like a drug. More of you doing whatever it is you are doing.

Coping Strategy
Keep Your Nose Clean or, "A clean nose is a happy nose".

This is especially useful for "scentsative" individuals.

Picking your nose is NOT a good idea for a variety of health reason. Keep it clean with water instead. Whenever you can, try to moisten your nostrils with a bit of water. Many people find that nasal membranes quickly become dry after smelling trigger molecules. Protect your molecule sensor by keeping it clean and clear and hydrated. Your nose is your air filter and a dirty air filter is a non-existent air filter.

As we all know, too much of "more" is often not a good thing.

Reactive Bodies should not be exposed to excessive glutamates! They already have hair trigger NMDA cells sensitized to open up the valve gates when stimulated. Excessive glutamates in the blood can sometimes trigger them into a hyper flared-up state.

The NMDA hypothesis offers a biological explanation that encompasses the wide variety of symptoms experienced by Reactive Body people. Anything from excessive trigger exposure through smell, touch or ingestion, to emotional shock can open the NDMA valves creating the characteristic bundle of sensitivities that go with it.

There was a famous experiment where a group of people who identified themselves as chemically sensitive were exposed to a wide variety of fragrances. Most of the subjects quickly reacted to ALL of them, even when natural pine and orange oils were introduced. Some then began reacting to "fresh" air. The researchers concluded that what they were seeing was a suggestion-based reaction, a psychosomatic condition. Had they understood the reality of living in a Reactive Body they may have reached an alternative conclusion.

Let's look at the same data this way:

Nearly all artificial scents/flavor concentrates are just 7% to 20% scent molecules. The rest is solvent. The most commonly used solvents are alcohol and toluene. Knowing that nearly all the already chemically sensitive subjects could be triggering off of toluene, we could reasonably expect them all to enter into full-blown flare-ups where even natural aromas became painful.

Try snorting a little bit of water into each nostril. Water in the nose is generally pretty uncomfortable, so this will take some getting used to, but it's worth it. Once your nose is rehydrated you will want to blow it clean. I use this water sniffing coping strategy when I get exposed to dust or to strong petrochemical smells. It always helps me to reduce the chance of a flare-up.

This is the body's natural defense system kicking in and protecting it from over-exposure to the perceived toxic substance. And during a flare-up your body is telling you that NONE is the acceptable amount right now!

Chapter 4

Reactive Body / Reactive Mind

Learning to live with a Reactive Body and the Reactive Mind that goes with it is all about achieving balance. And balance requires awareness. You have to be strong and centered every day so you can pay attention. You need to hear and interpret the signals your body is giving you.

When we feel panicked or claustrophobic it feels like we are not fully in our bodies; we begin to jump out of our skin. It is as if we are in such a hurry to leave this moment we get ahead of ourselves. Centering puts you back where you belong, firmly inside yourself, at one with your body. This is a very important and special tool you can use your entire life. It will calm you and allow you to face life from a centered place inside. Sounds simple right? Unfortunately, it usually is not. Practice! Practice! Practice!

Staying on the Ball

Imagine a ball, a big red ball, about 3 feet in diameter. Now imagine a sea lion balancing on that ball. See it? The sea lion is doing pretty well. Now imagine a clown collar around the sea lion balancing on that red ball, and imagine her wearing a funny hat, like they wear at birthday parties. Still on the ball? Cool.

Now put a row of old fashioned bicycle horns fixed to a shiny stand in front of her. Let's have that sea lion play a tune while balancing on the ball wearing a clown collar and funny hat. Still on the ball? I bet it's getting wobbly. Imagine that a car stops in front of our musical sea lion and a whole crowd of clowns get out and start marching around clashing cymbals and playing out of tune. The sea lion falls off the ball.

Now imagine that YOU are that balancing sea lion. When you fall off YOUR ball of sanity, how will you react? Some people fall off into anger and violence. Some fall into despair. Some fall into a manic/panic. Others become clumsy and self-conscious. And some just "gotta go" (as in right now!).

However you tend to fall off your ball, draping yourself in guilt and self-recrimination just makes it that much more difficult to climb back on. You are going to fall off your ball. Get over it! And while you're at it, get back on the ball! Mastering the art and science of living in your reactive body means mastering yourself. **And that means playing as best you can with the cards you have in your hand right now.**

Think of it as a learning experience: "How can I push the envelope a little further before I fall off my ball? How can I jump back onto it faster – maybe so fast that no one even notices that I slipped off? And how can I strengthen my sense of humor so I don't have a big reaction the next time around?"

No matter how you handle it, falling off your ball has an emotional exhaustion component that can really put a cramp in your day.

You need to deal with it immediately by:

1) Reducing Stimulation (see the coping strategy).

2) Drinking a bunch of good, filtered, non-plastic water.

3) Taking a quick tonic like fresh squeezed juice or whatever you can find that has an antidote effect for you.

4) Resting. Put yourself in the most peaceful and plant filled place you can find.

5) Forgiving yourself. Realize that the human experience is universal and that you are just one in billions of humans who will come and go on this planet.

6) And most importantly: keeping your sense of humor and not panicking!

Coping Strategy
One Minute Meditation

Here's a quick exercise you can do to practice staying alert to the subtle clues all around you right now.

Start by doing fingers and toes.

Now take three deep breaths in and out of your nose. Make each breath a little deeper than the one before. Relax your chest when you reach the top of the inhalation so your outbreath is almost a sigh.

Mentally let all your tensions and all of your discomforts blow out with every breath. Tell those tensions and discomforts to forever vanish and never reappear.

After taking these three deep, sighing breaths you will have a moment when your body has taken in enough oxygen and you will not have to breathe again for a few seconds. This is a very special moment.

Setting your cares and judgments aside, put all of our attention into your hearing. Start by trying to hear sounds that are very close. Now push out with your hearing awareness until you can hear faint sounds coming from far away. Further and further you go until all you can hear is the sound of the next breath your body is forcing you to take. Take a deep breath and feel your fingers, feel your toes again. Feeling better? And it only took one minute.

Except for your reading lamp, turn off every light in the room, or even the house, right now. I'll wait. Finished yet?

Now, don't you feel better?

When company comes over I like to turn on every blessed light in the house. It seems to make people more comfortable to enter a well-lit area upon arrival. Once everyone settles down I discreetly turn off every other light. I sometimes do this when visiting with friends. They think I'm some kind of eco-nut saving electricity all the time, but saving money and energy is just a favorable byproduct of reducing glare-stress wherever I go.

Pay ongoing attention to glare and to lighting and to how different types of lighting make you feel. Experiment with changing light bulb types, wattages and color spectrums. Find out what makes you feel best. Take out those old, buzzy, inefficient, fluorescent fixtures and replace them with quiet, energy efficient lights with fuller spectrum bulbs. The bluish light of fuller spectrum fluorescent bulbs will seem dimmer than the full yellow/white brightness of the old incandescent bulbs, but you will feel calmer around them.

I like the incandescent-like covered compact fluorescent bulbs. These are enclosed so you cannot see the spirals and they emit a really nice light. I especially like the reliable MAXLITE bulbs for balancing brightness, spectrum and electrical savings. Even though you are turning off every other light, keep plenty of brightness on your work areas.

We replaced all the old fluorescent tubes in the offices of the organic soap factory where I work each day. At first everyone complained. But once they got used to them, it was obvious that everyone felt calmer and far less burned out by the end of the day. No one ever complains anymore.

Now pay attention to the sounds in your space. Turn off TVs whenever and wherever possible, and limit their use to 120 minutes a day (including watching a movie). Some people like to keep televisions on for background noise when they are sleeping or going about their chores. This is not a good idea. Not for you, not for children and pets, not for your plants – just not good. Use a fan for background noise and air circulation or try a soothing sound generator or a pump bubbling in an aquarium. Try listening to Public Radio and to different types of music from all the cultures of the world instead of the television.

Any light or noise that makes you tense or stressed or reactive – just turn it off! If you can't, use earplugs, sunglasses, floppy and brim hats, plants and curtains to reduce light and sound stimulation wherever you are.

A scientist changes one variable and observes it effect,

and you should follow the same formula. Change only one thing at a time. Start with the lighting. Look for subtle changes in your mood, degree of aches or pain level, testiness, headache, eye ache, manic impulses. Don't jump to a conclusion after one test. Go back to the beginning and try again. For example, if you suspect that the lights in your workplace are tiring your eyes and debilitating you, wear a baseball cap to work for a few days. Without expecting any result, see if there is one.

If your co-workers start making comments like, "Well aren't you the cheerful one for a change!" then you might be onto something. The Universe will give you the information if you know what you are looking for. You just have to stay open to listen for the message.

Chapter 5

Triggers and Flare-Ups

A Reactive Body having a **flare-up** is not a pretty site. One might experience rashes, nausea, dizziness, achiness, fatigue, swelling, and sweating; or become forgetful and confused and have difficulty staying focused. It is possible to feel especially manic or ADHD; or both! Anxiety and panic often accompany the beginning of a big time flare-up.

Once you get a low immune system buffer warning from day to day trigger exposure (i.e. headache, general weakness, sore throat, skin, aromatic, sound or light sensitivities) you can implement one of the many Coping Strategies outlined in this book to help keep yourself together.

What pushes a person into a flare-up?

Unfortunately, there are lots of things that can trigger a flare-up. Some common stressors are noise; interruptions in diet, routine, or environment; lack of sleep; excessive alcohol consumption; recreational drug use; traveling and returning from traveling; PTSD triggers; fragrances; fake flavorings; drinking water or other liquids in plastic bottles for extended periods of time (estrogen mimicking phthalate poisoning); pesticide exposure; new construction

> **Coping Strategy**
> **10 Second Centering**
> **– Fingers and Toes**
>
> Place your awareness inside of your fingertips. Feel them from the inside out. Hold this awareness for a few seconds.
>
> Feel your fingers.
>
> Now feel your toes.
>
> Take a deep, slow breath through your nose, paying attention to the air you are drawing in.
>
> When you have comfortably expanded your lungs let the air out of itself, like a sigh. You will feel things click into place, like everything is as it should be.

off-gassing; new car smell; tires; and paint drying. It's as if some predisposed bodies get filled up with whatever they are exposed to on a daily basis. The slightest whiff of it again, especially when in a flared up state, and the body begins to squirm!

Biological, molecular, topical, or emotional inflammation makes everything worse. Inflammation can trigger you into a reactive flare-up state. In fact, I would even state that irritation creates inflammation, which CAUSES reactive flare-ups. That leads to inevitably to collapse and exhaustion, to reduced immune system buffer and a cascade of other potentially negative results.

Having a Reactive Body may force you to eliminate many postindustrial formulations such as those used in paint, surface cleaners, body care products, fuels and plastics. This is especially difficult when everyone around you does not seem to notice that there is even a problem. Perhaps instead we should be grateful that our own Reactive Bodies force us to get away from those very molecules that can potentially hurt us!

EMF's, or Electromagnetic Frequencies, are not your friend either. Things that did not exist in the day-to-day world we evolved to live in (like all these radio and micro waves) are being thrown around the planet as if they were guaranteed proven safe in multi-generational studies. Our bodies are in part electrical and we are affected by radiation fields created by high voltage power generation and transmission, cell phones and towers, electrical metering devices, Wi-Fi transmission devices, long airplane rides and baby monitors (for starters). Reactive Bodies need to avoid excess EMF exposure as much as is possible. Actually,

Wasn't that nice? If you haven't done it yet, try Fingers and Toes now, before you go on. It only takes a couple of breaths to feel better.

The hardest part is remembering to do this at least once a day. Do it more often when you are feeling especially reactive.

everybody does, but the Reactive Bodies are the ones getting told the message the loudest.

I will tell you that flare-ups ARE manageable with practice. Here is your basic management game plan:

1) Soothe symptoms with *inflammation reducers* and *coping strategies.*

2) Identify and reduce and eliminate *trigger molecules* as much as you can.

3) Build up your *immune system buffer* so you can deal with inadvertent exposure.

4) Rotate your *tonics* and *antidotes* (which we'll get into later) to build up your medicine chest while steadily increasing the nutritional value of everything you ingest and eliminating processed foods and empty calories.

Coping Strategy
Check it Thrice

When working with any variable, first make the change, then look for any observable relevant difference. And then go back to the beginning and start again.

Let's say that you have always suspected that your kitchen light makes you uncomfortable. As an experiment, you might tape the kitchen light switch in the off position and use a number of small wattage bulbs in shaded lamps instead. Maybe try a few unscented beeswax candles. Go back and forth three times between lighting schemes carefully and dispassionately (that means that you try not to have a pre-conceived opinion as to the outcome) and look for real, relevant and repeatable data about how your body reacts or doesn't react to the change. The best thing you can do to facilitate this is to keep a log of things you do and do not react to, and anything that you notice that makes you feel "clearer" or "cleaner".

Let's say you have changed your most obviously obnoxious bulbs and turned off every other light. Your TV is off but you still feel like crap anyway. Your body is achy and you wonder for the third time this week if you are coming down with something. By now you are probably wondering if the bookstore will give you your money back for this useless book.

Then your housemate pours some cleaning glop into hot water to do the dishes.

And your head starts to explode.

This is where you calmly run for fresh air.

The solution to pollution is dilution.

That fresh lemony scent that many people seem to find so appealing apparently increases your Reactive Body symptoms. You suddenly realize that *every* time someone does the dishes you get a headache. Take a half second to congratulate yourself on finding new relevant data. Then quickly open a window and maybe a door to achieve **cross-ventilation**. Put yourself in the path of the fresh incoming air. If you feel better immediately you then have further confirmed the reliability of your data.

LESS of something that is bad for you is better than MORE of it. I would rather be a little hungry than lot hungry, and a little achy rather than a lot achy. Dilution is a coping strategy. It will help you to get through your day. Your real goal however is to eliminate, as much as possible, the triggers that set off your Reactive Body.

Quiet the mind, quiet the body. Read the clues all around you. To be a great molecular detective you need to quiet yourself inside so you can read the subtle clues that your body is sending you.

Chapter 6

Tonics and Antidotes

Tonics are anything that helps increase your overall resistance to external irritants, or what I like to call the **Immune System Buffer**. Your Immune System Buffer is the amount of good molecules you have in reserve at any given moment to push back against the bad-for-you molecules. Tonics work in a variety of ways and metabolic pathways. That is the beauty of using them; you get to enhance and support different parts of your immune system over time. **Antidotes** are tonics that work so well for you that they can quickly help to stave off a **flare-up**. As every Reactive Body is different, you'll have to put your Sherlock Homes hat back on to find out what your specific tonics and antidotes are, but I can give you some suggestions where to start.

Water

Water is your first and most important tonic. When you take good water and oxygenate it so it mimics water from a babbling, bubbling brook it briefly becomes something more: it becomes medicine. To oxygenate your water, first make sure your faucet has an aerator screen on it. The aerator breaks up the flow of the water, which puts more air into the water. Then run the water until it is good and cold. Take a pint glass and rinse it in the cold water to chill it. Then let the water drop as far as it can so that it picks up as much oxygen as possible. Drink the water down fast while it is still full of bubbles.

Oxygenated water can make you feel energetic and clear-headed and put you in a good mood, even if you were not feeling so well before drinking it. If you notice yourself slipping into a Reactive flare-up, downing a pint of fresh, unadulterated water might just be enough to calm those feelings of hypersensitivity down.

Without water we cannot have life, and without clean, non-infected and non-chemical treated water we cannot have GREAT health. However, all kinds of nasty-nasties want to set up shop in your water and sewer pipes right now. Without regular chemical flushing, the population would be open to a wide variety of potential ills. The thing is that when we use anti-life substances like antibiotics, antimicrobials, fungicides, pesticides and herbicides, we are also harming ourselves, our children, our pets and our grandchildren. You want the pipes to be disinfected regularly, but you do not want to ingest those chloramines and chlorines. This presents a very good case for drinking carbon-filtered water, especially if you are connected to a municipal or district water system. I suggest putting a filter on your showerhead, too.

Securing a steady source of water that does not smell

like plastic is vitally important. Glass is the best container, but do the best you can. #2 HDPE plastic or cellulose products are acceptable for use by Reactive Bodies. Remember: the clearer the plastic and the more flexible, the more phthalates the product contains. These are believed to be estrogen mimickers and endocrine disruptors. I'm not crazy about the coating on milk cartons, either. If your family drinks milk and you live in an area where local, organic milk in returnable glass bottles is available, I recommend you switch immediately.

Air and Sunlight

Fresh, clean air is a tonic in this crazy polluted world we call the 21st century. And breathing natural aromas may have some health benefits as you absorb tonic molecules from the air.

Sunlight is a powerful health tonic

Coping Strategy Not Breathing

I have friend who works with toxic chemicals every day. He tries to be good about it, but does not always wear a mask when he should. I asked him how he could even be alive with all his exposure to volatile solvent molecules every day.

"That's easy," he replied. "I just don't breathe."

He has trained himself so that the second he senses a trigger molecule he stops inhaling. This gives him a few seconds to finish what he's doing and then go for air.

When you feel that you have to breathe in - breathe out instead. It will buy you another few seconds to get out of harm's way and into fresh clean air.

for humans, too! Seasonally Affected Disorder (SAD) can erode your Immune System Buffer. SAD is a mild seasonal depression due to a profound lack of sunlight in the eyeballs. On those precious few sunny days in winter, I make sure to get some sunlight in my eyeballs whenever I can. When you are driving in the wintertime try lowering the window, taking off your sunglasses and turning up the heat. How about lingering in the sun as you enter and leave buildings? Whatever it takes to get some sunlight working its way down that optic nerve and stimulating the your pineal gland.

Foods

Water may be most the most important tonic, but it's not the only one! Many everyday things can be tonics. Most aromatic herbs and spices are powerful tonics that you can use in your day-to-day life. The more the better! The list of tonic worthy foods is long and varied, which is good because that keeps your life interesting. Bulk bins (weigh your own) at co-ops are an excellent way to get nutrition dense foods at lower prices. It is best for Reactive Bodies to buy **Certified Organic** foods whenever possible. Certified Organic means Audited Natural. Other than growing it yourself, organic certification is your best chance at buying clean (chemical free) products. Look for the name of the certifier below the company's contact information. If these things are not shown (they are often on the lower right hand side of the label) you probably are not looking at a genuine certified organic product.

Here is a very partial list of potential tonics you can eat every day:

- Fresh, colorful, pesticide-free vegetables, fruit, berries and grains

- Cold, expeller-pressed, fresh organic vegetable oils

- Omega Essential Fatty Acid (EFA) sources, like free range eggs, cracked flax and hemp seed oils, and deep water fish

- Fresh squeezed organic lemonade, orange juice, and other juice blends that agree with you

- Homemade sauerkraut and pickled vegetables

- All spices and most herbs, often containing astonishing concentrated antioxidant healing power

- Organic organ meats, like liver

Get in the habit of washing fruits and vegetables in diluted natural castile liquid soap based products to remove oily surface sprays, bacteria, and molds like *candida albicans*. *Candida* is a very common mold that lives on wild fruits and berries. You can make your own fruit and vegetable wash by using about 5% organic liquid soap in clean water.

Soap formulas vary and so does water, so you'll need to adjust the amount of soap in your mix as you go. If it is too foamy, dilute. If there aren't any suds or a minimal amount, add more soap. Simple! In fact, I consider real soap to be kind of a Wonder Substance.

Soap is natural. Soap-like molecules are found in nature and in your own bodies right now. There are over a dozen plant species that will create a mild foam if you work them well in warm water. Your own body creates saponins, natural soap-like substances to help break up fats and digest oily/fatty foods. Synthetic chemical detergents are never naturally occurring on the planet. Soap molecules are one of the good guys found in nature, are safe and nontoxic, and effective to use in our day to day lives, but I digress... I am the Soapman after all!

Black and Green Teas vs Coffee: Quick! Which tea is better for you, black or green?

If you have a favorite, that's great. Near as I can tell, BOTH forms of the dried *camellia sinensis* plant are good for you. If I were a tea drinker I would make a blend and get the full benefit. But I am not a tea drinker. I prefer very dark and oily organic coffee; fresh, unsweetened, and black. My wife's black tea contains antioxidants like quercitin. All that tea she drinks probably adds up to the caffeine in one cup of my brew, but hers may have added benefits for cardiovascular health, cancer prevention, and reducing the risk of diabetes.

Green tea provides similar benefits plus some real botanical goodies of polyphenols called catechins and epicatechins. These powerful antioxidants provide a cascade of positive effects on a wide range of systems in your body. Three cups a day is a really good idea for the Reactive Body. You're helping to reduce your risk for cancer, helping your arteries, and much more. If I were sick in bed, drinking three cups of green tea a day would definitely be part of my self-cure.

My organic coffee is not without a positive side, however. Those rich oils contain antioxidants, too, and seem to also have a positive effect against diabetes and rectal cancer. All good, as long as I stick to one coffee drink a day. More than that and the inflammatory effects of caffeine kick in, and for Reactive Bodies inflammation is THE enemy.

Vitamins and Herbs

Here are some of my favorites – what I consider nutritional gold!

Nutritional Yeast: This is a dry yeast powder similar to the nutrition packed yeast left at the bottom of beer brewing vessels. Pigs thrive on it and nutritional yeast is the basis for vitamin B pills. It is rich in micro minerals like selenium, which is important if you live and eat in a selenium poor agricultural area. This is good nutrition that can also

Immediately upon entering a new building, room, or situation, stop and take an awareness-filled breath through your nose and down into your chest. Smell the molecules in the air and scan for the ones that trigger you.

You will have to make a determination as to how long you can stay in that room (if at all).

There is a window over in the corner; will they let you open it?

Is there a balcony to stand on, feigning a long forgotten interest in astronomy?

help in staying healthy and calm. Sprinkle it onto eggs, into gravies, in vegetable juicing concoctions. Nutritional Yeast tastes incredible on popcorn – kind of like cheese!

Back in the Hippy Days I used to drink ¼ cup of nutritional yeast with a pinch of cayenne pepper every morning. I poured in 2/3 cup of very hot water and drank it down quickly. My face would get red from the niacin in it. This is natural and is called a niacin flush. We thought that it was good for us, and maybe it was, but if you are not ready for that flush you will think you are having an allergic reaction to the stuff. Try it with a half pinch of dried sea kelp for an extra trace mineral boost. If you take a lot of vitamins, eating Nutritional Yeast every day is a less expensive alternative for many of your daily pills.

Immune System Building Mushrooms like Rishi, Maitake,

Shiitake, Cordyceps, Turkey Tail, Chaga etc.: These are special mushrooms that grow on wood and break it down. They are not food, but they are extremely powerful tonics. Mushroom tonics supercharge and support your immune system. They are your allies when you are worn down by persistent illness. Some of these mushrooms work on the cells in your immune system. Chaga helps the mitochondria in your cells work more efficiently, giving you more energy. Tonic mushrooms work best when mixed together to help prevent illness and can shorten the time you are down when you do get sick. Take them as a powder in pill form, in a glycerin/maple syrup extract or as a tincture (steeped in alcohol). Your body will probably like having these mushrooms in it. I take them during Flu Season and when I am traveling or hit by plant and mold overload. They are all quite powerful. Be sure to rotate

Be sure to have an inhaler that works as a backup.

No matter how careful you are there will always be chance exposure to molecular triggers.

your mushroom tonics for maximum effectiveness and so you do not become dependent on them to feel strong. They work that well.

I learned this lesson the hard way. I took a Chaga concentrate in Ginseng tea for almost a year, once. I stopped taking it and within a few days I felt dried up, weak and empty. Because Chaga increases mitochondria functionality by up to 20%, I had nearly 20% more energy and élan. I did not get sick once the entire time I took the ginseng combination. However, because I stayed on it too long, getting off of it was too close to kicking a drug craving. You don't want to keep your system zinged up and then let it crash. Develop of full kit of tonics, rotate them every six weeks and keep yourself fresh for the next molecular assault you encounter.

Ginseng: Ginseng will help to boost you back up when you are worn down by immune system buffer destroying triggers. The active molecules in ginseng are water-soluble, so tea or powder works fine as a delivery system for this tonic herb. Ginseng is renowned as the (temporary) cure for men feeling a lack of libido. Like all tonics you don't want to stay on it forever.

Dong Quai: Dong Quai is an Asian herb that is the female equivalent of ginseng. It is a standard herbal ingredient in preparations for "women's troubles" especially when a temporary lack of libido is a factor. Dong Quai can help to boost you up when you flagging and run down. It is especially good for women but occasionally used by men in combination with other herbs. People are complicated, so do not use Dong Quai as a substitute for regular visits with a medical professional.

Vitamin C and the Bioflavonoid Family: In nature, vitamin C is always found in a bundle: a bioflavonoid complex. In the vitamin store it is usually sold as ascorbic acid – pure synthetic vitamin C. While synthetic vitamin C might be a good tonic to pick you back up when you are sagging, it is far better to get your vitamin C in a bundle. Several supplement formulators have told me that our bodies use vitamins in a group – the way they are found in nature. They told me that when we take a lot of a single vitamin, like vitamin C, we feel really good and clear for a while, but then the pill has perceivable diminishing benefits. They hypothesized that when we take individual vitamins out of their natural bundle, we actually create deficiencies as we use up our internal supply of the other factors in the group. If they are correct there is little long-term benefit to this type of dietary supplementation. (If you do take synthetic vitamin C, limit yourself to 300mg/day to reduce the risk of developing kidney stones.)

It is far better to enjoy freshly squeezed orange juice every day, taking in the whole healthy bundle of fresh, water soluble vitamins your body craves. Most orange juice, however, is far removed from freshly juiced. It is actually an engineered product, built from anything found in an orange or on its peel. Yuck. Will I grab whatever orange juice is around if that is the only tonic I can find at that moment and I am flagging? You bet! When you need to push back against the fog, you use what is nearby. However it is far better to squeeze fresh orange juice into your mouth than to get it in reconstituted form from a plastic bottle. Try mixing carrot juice with freshly squeezed orange juice. You will be surprised at how good it tastes, not to mention how clear-headed and energetic you will feel!

Vitamin E and the Tocopherol family: This group of molecules protects oils from going rancid. They are also really good for you too and especially for your heart and arteries. Since Reactive Bodies are prone to adrenal exhaustion (which eats up your arteries) this is a something you want to pay attention to.

When anti-oxidants (tonic-like vitamins and botanicals that neutralize the by-products of your metabolism) are working you can tell pretty quickly. You feel like someone went in and dusted the cobwebs out of your brain. Your mind works faster and you feel less run down and drained. You might feel like running or exercising for the first time in months.

Guide to some tonics with a specific result in mind

Sleeping Tonics: It is very important for Reactive Body people to keep a regular sleep/wake cycle so their immune system will function optimally. You may have to tweak your sleep pattern from time to time and need the occasional sleeping aid. Here two natural solutions:

Valerian (root): This is the plant that the active ingredient in Valium was isolated from. Drink some light tea while reading in bed. Works great!

Melatonin (available in health food stores and on-line): Used briefly and sparingly in low doses, melatonin can be a very useful tool when you need to reset your internal clock.

Tonics for Depressing Feelings and Thoughts

It is best not to dwell on obsessive thoughts. Train yourself to say something positive, to find what is good in the moment and to stop thinking about yourself. There is not a lot in life that trains us to keep ourselves happy by looking for and accentuating the positive, but if you practice coming back to center every time you notice yourself dwelling on things that make you feel bad you will be able to take back your life. Here are some nontoxic herbal ways reported to help:

Chocolate: REAL chocolate is tonic. Its high anti-oxidant content basically makes it a super food. It's also makes people feel warm and snugly and full of wellbeing.

And the downside of this is what? Practicing moderation. Practice! Practice!

Treat yourself to a pound of real organic powdered Dutch chocolate powder (co-op store staple). Mix it well with 50% good sugar and nice spices like cinnamon.

St. John's Wart: This is the king of herbs for transient depression issues. However, it is really only effective for 6-8 weeks. After that, many people report only nominal value from using it. You can up the dosage over time, but the fact is that this is a tonic for transient issues. It is not for the treatment of long-term clinic depression. Use a standardized extract with dosage calculated for your body mass and increase the dosage slowly over a two-month period. Then try something else like a Vermont ski vacation and a new aerobics tape combined with fresh juices.

Antidotes

Antidotes are emergency first aid for stressed out bodies and emotions. I put them in a different category than the tonics you take on a daily basis to boost your immune system buffer that you need to rotate every six weeks. They may in fact be the same substances, just taken to quell a flare-up rather than as a daily health aid. Since you want help fast, I recommend water based molecules, such as unfiltered natural juices and teas.

There was a television show from 1985 to 1992 about a spy-type guy named MacGyver. He was unusual in that he refused to carry a weapon. Instead he used common sense and his knowledge of chemistry and physics to get out of whatever pickle he happened to find himself in. **He used what was around him to make what he needed to solve the issue of the moment.** You need to be able to "MacGyver" your way out of trouble when you find yourself in a Reactive situation, but are without your usual bundle of plant based medicines.

Here's an example:

After traveling by plane for eight hours, I found myself in an airport at 2am completely fried. I was hungry and toxified and on the verge of a breakdown. If ever someone needed an antidote this was it. Somehow I had nothing with me and every store and restaurant in the airport was closed, except one. The all night pizza place was still going strong. I was completely broke after traveling, but I went through my stuff and scraped together enough coin for a slice of pizza. Being lactose intolerant, I had them remove the cheese and bring me a side container filled with oregano. Fortunately they were generous, and I put a good 2 heaping tablespoons worth onto that pizza. Oregano is a powerful tonic herb with strong antibacterial and antioxidant properties. Down in the bottom of my daypack I found a couple of beat up packages of vitamin C drink, which I mixed with water and drunk down. Once again clear headed and strong, fed and watered, and brought back to life, I made it safely home in reasonably good spirits.

By knowing what my antidotes were, I was able to save myself from a serious flair-up. And YOU need to know what YOUR body needs in these kinds of situations so you can avoid a meltdown too.

Un-Tonics

Things that are not found in nature are almost never tonics. Things that make you fuzzy headed, sleepy and listless are not tonics. Bad popular drinks and bad modern lighting are definitely not tonics. Plastic and petrochemicals are not tonics, and they contaminate food and liquids stored in them. The more highly processed a food is the less tonic remains in there for you to add to your immune system buffer.

Artificial scents are no more tonics than artificial colors are. Glues are not tonics either, and they might off-gas into the contents of laminated food service cartons.

The nonstick coating on food service to-go containers is not a tonic, neither is the remain-on-the-plate surface disinfectant used by most restaurants in their automatic dishwashers or on bar glasses. Ask your favorite restaurant if they disinfect using heat only or using heat and chemicals.

The de-limer they use in the dishwasher to make those plates sparkle is not your friend either. Your waiter will not know about hidden restaurant chemicals but the owner might. If it is a national franchise you can be sure the full Monty of chemical sanitary protection is being used for THEIR personal liability protection.

Some things are tonics on moderation like good coffee, but are inflammatory in higher doses as when caffeine makes you feel anxious. Alcohol comes to mind here too. Reactive Bodies can scarce afford the liver damage or free radical overload that comes from a night of binge drinking. But some home brewed beer or organic wine can work wonders at the end of a weary day AND provide needed tonic molecules.

Chapter 7

Everything Should be Medicine

Or: Everything that goes into your mouth or touches your skin MUST be medicine.

I cannot guarantee that if you follow this rule that you will live twenty active years longer, or that you will always look far younger than your actual age or that you will have fewer flare-ups. But what I CAN guarantee is that if you treat yourself and the eco-system that supports you poorly, it will be a hekuva lot harder to make these good things happen!

You might be thinking, "How can EVERYTHING that goes on me or in me be MEDICINE?" The answer is pretty simple: Make the healthiest choice possible every time. Medicine in this context means everything that makes you stronger.

Reactive Bodies should almost NEVER eat processed foods, drink processed or plastic bottled fluids or use mass-market personal care and cleaning products. For one thing, we need lots of nutrition to recover from every-day minor flare-ups and close encounters of the molecular kind. For another, we can't be investing ALL our waking time analyzing whether or not we might have a sodium bromate sensitivity or if it was the GMO corn used that set us off.

Just choose the healthiest option you can and continue to evolve and learn from there.

Look for local, natural, organic products – the closer to original form the better. Support your local Farmers Markets, Co-ops, CSAs and Food Buying Clubs. Eat meat? Choose local, grass fed or organic animals as much as possible. You might be allowed to keep a few chickens, even in urban areas. Like beer and wine? There are plenty of healthy choices sold in glass to choose from, or learn to make your own. Start a vegetable garden or even just a little sprout and wheatgrass farm on your kitchen counter. It's fun, it's hip, and it just plain makes good common sense to eat fresh, local, and organic foods. You should always eat a wide variety of fresh and colorful foods. You don't want to have to take a million pills a day to get all your vitamins.

"Colorful foods?" you might be asking.

A-yup! The good stuff – the medicine stuff – is often found in the colorful (and sometimes bitter) portions of plants. Bright colors in plant foods indicate flavonoids; anti-oxidants; vitamins; chlorophyll, which contains magnesium; carotenoids; and many other yummy, healthy, botanical goodies. Plants you see every day produce anti-inflammation and anti-tumor molecules, essential fatty acids (oils you need every day) and things we are just now pinning down for maintaining optimum health.

Nearly all edible plants and herbs become medicine when they are fresh, colorful and full of Life Energy. A varied and interesting diet full of colorful plants and whole grains (and good animal products if you choose), makes SO MUCH SENSE that it's hard to imagine why ANYONE would support the Mass Food industries. I am quite sure that we were tricked into it.

Once you are used to good wholesome food and fresh clean water, processed food and drink has zero attraction. But if your household rarely eats a fresh vegetable and microwaves most of their meals, you are bound to come up against some resistance with a change in the food routine. There are some clever ways to change your family's habits, though. Run out of white sugar regularly, but leave honey and real maple syrup available and easily dispensable. Buy a bulk tub of organic smooth peanut butter and forget to buy the sweet/salty, processed stuff. Make the kids buy junk food with money that they earned themselves. Involve them in making granola or yogurt or grinding grain or growing sprouts. These are real life lesson opportunities and it teaches them age-old survival skills. You will survive the "hippy" comments just fine.

I recommend you **take a cooking class** to kick-start the process. The best way to combat processed engineered food is with yummy healthy food fresh from the oven! Win 'em with wow. When they question why the sudden onset of new dishes and experiments you can blame it on the class. "Just trying out some techniques I learned in in the cooking class I'm taking." That way they won't suspect that you are trying to save you and your family's lives in small ways every day.

All kidding aside, trying to cook for a Reactive Body can be very tough. I cannot comment on what will work for you and what will not, but I can give you some good tips to help you find a balanced and interesting diet that will neither make you prone to a flare-up nor bore you to tears.

Let's take this process in levels:

Level 1

Start by eliminating every food-like substance that contains artificial colors and flavors. Flavors are identical to fragrances in more instances than you can imagine and can trigger a flare-up in sensitized individuals. The secondary benefit of this diet is that you avoid a lot of nasty chemicals in processed food. (This is essentially the Feingold Diet™.)

Introduce rice and curry dishes, ethnic foods from around the world (other than pizza), exotic grains, vegetables, and interesting new meat dishes if you are omnivorous. Reduce coffee, drink more green tea and take probiotics for three weeks every six months. That's *probiotics* as in the opposite of *antibiotics*. If they give you gas, that could indicate that you are lactose sensitive. Some probiotics are formulated with *inulin*, a sugar found in Jerusalem Artichokes. This is terrific stuff for growing good probiotic stomach flora, but some people just can't digest the stuff. Their bodies lack the enzyme to break it down. Do some experiments to find out what works for YOU.

Level 2

Now that you have cleaned up your food act, you can really pay attention to fine tuning and optimizing your diet. Look for things that make you bloated and gassy; that give you a migraine, diarrhea or hemorrhoids. Try eating one thing at time so as not to confuse the issue. Conduct the same experiment **three times** to isolate and confirm specific ingredient sensitivities if you are unsure.

Pay attention to your body and take notes. When you do eliminate something, do it seriously and thoroughly. You will also want to pay attention to what foods and spices are **tonics** for you, so stay alert!

Level 3

Try adding the Eat Right 4 Your Blood Type diet to your eating system. (There is a book by that name you can check out.) For many people this is the final fine tuning they need to get their bellies right. It is amazing how many things you just do not like will be on your "bad" list. Reactive Bodies definitely need to pay attention to blood type dietary considerations.

Level 4

A wise person once said, "The superior person pays attention to what goes into their mouth; and to what comes out of their mouth."

This is where you want to be living your life. You now have a good understanding of what works and does not work for your body and blood type. At Level 4, everything you ingest is medicine. Everything is a tonic. If you ingest something bad, you learn your lesson and move along. You enjoy a good level of health and wellbeing, and you do not need a lot of doctors telling you what and what not to do. You rarely take chemical medications because your whole life is medicine.

This is the level where your spirituality blossoms. You surround yourself with people who are not toxic to your emotional stability; people who make you feel good about yourself and your unique mental/emotional/biological perspective. You stop being preoccupied with yourself and your issues, begin to volunteer, and help others on their personal journeys. Remember that almost everyone you meet was traumatized, too, often by things you could never imagine. Try to be compassionate and always operate from a place of integrity.

Nontoxic Skin Care and Cleaning Solutions

I've devoted the past 22 years of my working life to developing nontoxic solutions for topical applications. Please visit www.vtsoap.com for more information and for real products that you can use without pain. Rather than focus on all the BAD ingredients, here are the natural solutions that you need:

Skin and face soap: Most Reactive Bodies also have reactive skin. Use handmade bar soaps with a 3%+/- superfat content. This means that the bars will be extremely mild and moisturizing. Palm oil based soaps can be especially mild when formulated properly. Avoid strong essential oils unless you are killing body fungus.

Moisturizers: Use non-water based moisturizers i.e. salves and balms. These are oilier and take longer to soak into your skin but they are your best bet for nontoxic moisturizing.

Sanitizers: Use alcohol and essential oil based sanitizers to kill germs. The ingredient carbomer is used to gel alcohol for hand sanitizers. This ingredient is very drying to sensitive skin. Straight alcohol is actually easier on your hands.

Underarm Deodorant: Avoid most of these products. Even so called natural ones are often primarily propylene glycol (anti-freeze). Vermont Soap makes an excellent certified organic underarm stick. Weleda makes a nice spray product that works, too.

Chemicals to avoid: Artificial scents and colors, detergents (ends with "ate" and "eth" as in Laureth and Laurly sulfates), triclosan, carbomer, BHT, butyl paraben; anything you do not actually know to be safe.

Good ingredients: Aloe Vera (NOT Aloe Vera gel), shea butter (when it is organic, unrefined and fresh) organic olive oil (much more soothing than regular olive oil) and nearly ALL organic vegetable oils, bee products, glycerin (NOT glycerin soaps), vitamin E, probiotics (inside and out), organic corn starch (NOT regular GMO cornstarch), Epsom Salts (magnesium source), sea salt, and baking soda (NOT from mined minerals!). *Note: people react to good ingredients too!*

Cleaning products: Now that you have made everything that goes in your mouth or touches your skin a medicine, you don't want to jeopardize that with harsh cleaning products. Use Castile liquid soap for general cleaning. (Visit vtsoap. com to learn more about this too.) Castile soap based foamers and spray cleaners work great and when done right are mild and effective. I also recommend Bon Ami for bathroom cleaning. It is cheap, natural and scentless.

Final Thoughts

I've been practicing these methods for 20 years, and still need to stay alert and practice being a molecular Sherlock Holmes every day. Because of my vigilance I rarely need chemical medicines or MDs and enjoy generally excellent health.

THIS is how you survive out there in the artificial environment that hypnotizes people into believing they have found the Good Life. But the medical numbers belay that myth. Obesity, diabetes, cancer, immune system breakdown diseases, and Reactive Bodies – these are NOT the signs of a healthy, long-term, sustainable, holistic approach to crafting our civilization.

When a society allows itself to be run by sociopaths, well – the evidence is all around us: cancer rates over 70%; air, water, and food poisoned; children all ADHD most of the time. Be happy that you have a Reactive Body that tells you in ways you have to be a zombie not to hear: "This

The Oasis Effect

Practice living your life as if you are an oasis in the desert. Be a source of life and sustenance to those you encounter. Gently influence others away from bad habits, especially if those habits involve triggers for you. Provide convenient healthy alternatives. In this way you will make your environment less toxic.

stuff is not good for you!"

It's obviously not good for the people around you either. But I will ask you – no, I will PLEAD with you – not to try to change the bad habits of those around you. You are making a thoughtful choice; an effort to clean up your act; to achieve a balance. You are working to find the elusive meaning of "natural" in the modern world. Your kids, your parents, your soul mate and your best friend may be the greatest people in the world, but they did not choose to make this journey yet. It is very easy to "turn off" the people around you that you care about, but it is much easier to make these necessary lifestyle changes when you have support from the people you love.

Your commitment here is to live a conscious life. By paying attention to the molecules, the details, and the clues around you, you will learn and understand more and more about the world and about yourself each and every day. By optimizing and moderating your activities and intakes, you will be in a better position to retain vitality and health throughout your life. And THIS is the essential message of this book.

All the Best!

Vocabulary of Your Reactive Body

(In no particular order)

Reactive Body: An individual who is physically and/or emotionally reactive to specific trigger molecules in the air, food, water, petrochemical products and body care products.

Immune System Buffer (ISB): The amount of resistance you have at any moment to fend off exposure to trigger molecules found in the above.

Flare-Up: What happens when a Reactive Body is exposed to trigger molecules with a rundown ISB. This book hypothesizes that during a flare-up one enters into a hypersensitive state which is characterized by a dramatic increase in the amperage of the electricity allowed through the nerves, and a heightened sensitivity/ reactivity to one's immediate environment. During this time there is an increased susceptibility to acquiring new environmental triggers.

Trigger: A molecule common in your environment that you have acquired sensitivity to. Many (but not all) triggers are synthetic.

Tonic: Anything that restores your ISB.

Antidote: Strong tonics that your body loves. Keep them handy; they can bring you back from the edge of a flare-up.

NMDA cells: "Dimmer Switch" cells that turn the amperage running through your nerves up or down. Triggered by calcium and glutamates.

Natural: As close to original form as is feasible and effective. Natural means using the molecular kit we inherited – not the one we invented– as best we can.

Coping Strategy: Simple techniques to help Reactive Bodies get through their day successfully and productively.

Key Phrase: A predetermined code you use with the people close to you to indicate that you are close to a flare up. My code phrase is, "Shit! I gotta get out of here!"

Larry Plesent is a writer, philosopher, soap maker, restaurateur, gardener and grandfather, living and working in the Green Mountains of Vermont.

Learn more at www.vermontsoap.com

Made in the USA
Middletown, DE
13 June 2015